POCKET IMAGES

Victorian
Nottingham

Mansfield Road, 1895

POCKET IMAGES

Victorian Nottingham

Michael Payne

NONSUCH

To Sarah and Roger

First published 1992
This new pocket edition 2007
Images unchanged from first edition

Nonsuch Publishing Limited
Cirencester Road, Chalford
Stroud, Gloucestershire, GL6 8PE
www.nonsuch-publishing.com

Nonsuch Publishing is an imprint of NPI Media Group

British Library Cataloguing in Publication Data.
A catalogue record for this book is available from the British Library.

ISBN 978-1-84588-425-3

Typesetting and origination by NPI Media Group
Printed in Great Britain

Contents

Workmen at Mapperley Brickyards.

Introduction

Like many late Victorians, Edwin Gordon was an enthusiast for the comparatively new and intricate art of photography. At that time it was a difficult process even to take the simplest picture. The negatives were on glass plates, which were carried in a heavy box, the camera had to be held still on a tripod, and all three items had to be transported on location.

When my mother, Dorothy Payne, died in 1988, I found a large number of glass negatives and hundreds of photographs taken by her father, Edwin Gordon, between 1890 and 1912. She will be seen on many of the photographs as the little girl in the middle distance, and she often described how she and her mother carried the photographic equipment on many country walks. Edwin developed and printed the photographs in his own small darkroom. The essential safety light was achieved by placing a large sheet of red glass over the entire window, so that he could only work when it was daylight outside. His internal light source was a spirit lamp, and by modern standards the process was long and cumbersome.

Later Edwin turned to stereoscopic photography, which can only be enjoyed by one viewer at a time, but he obtained some incredibly realistic three-dimensional images which, of course, have had to be printed in two dimensions in this book.

Edwin's plate camera was a Sanderson Field Camera dated 1890, with a shutter speed of between 1/2 and 1/100 second and an aperture of f6.5–f64. He took the stereoscopic photographs with a Blair Camera Stereo Hawkeye Model No. 2, made in 1910. This had a fixed aperture and a twin shutter speed of 1 second and 1/100 second.

The most exciting find is the collection of Goose Fair photographs, which are some of the earliest known, dating to between 1899 and 1912. Particularly interesting are the shots of bioscope sideshows, which would have been the first cinemas in Nottingham.

Most of Edwin's photographs had remained undisturbed since his death in 1929, and no more than a dozen of them had been labelled in any way. About half a dozen appeared in the *Nottingham Evening Post* 'Do you Remember?' series, and later found their way into the Iliffe and Baguley *Victorian Nottingham* books.

With the encouragement of Sheila Cook and Dorothy Ritchie at the Local Studies Library of the Central Library, this book has come into being, and I particularly wish to thank them for their assistance and also allowing me to supplement the book with photographs of central Nottingham from the Nottingham Historical Film Unit Collection compiled by Richard Iliffe and Wilfred Baguley, which is in the Local History Library. With one exception, Brewhouse Yard on page 113, all the other photographs are by Edwin Gordon.

In many ways this collection must resemble a family album, but at the same time I hope it will be of general interest as a record of Nottingham at a time of great change and expansion.

Edwin was typical of many upwardly mobile men of his time in that he began his married life living in central Nottingham. As he became more prosperous he removed in 1892 to the 'New' West Bridgford, and then after a few years decided on the more spacious north of the city made accessible by the new electric tram system.

The fact that emerges over and over again from his photographs, is the way the city has been changed by the needs of transport. First the widening of narrow medieval streets for trading purposes, then the staggering upheavals with the arrival of the railway; not long after came the demands of the electric tram, and finally the voracious motor car.

At the same time it is sobering to see how many grand schemes lasted for so short a time, particularly Victoria Station and the Great Central Line. The building of these landmarks took a monumental effort by comparatively primitive means, and yet had a life of less than seventy years.

Has the destruction of the past been worse in Nottingham than in any other English town? Probably not. Mercifully, we must be grateful for the preservation of such buildings as Severn's, Brewhouse Yard, the Theatre Royal and Green's Windmill. Yet there is much to mourn. Lack of imagination and planning accounts for some regrettable acts of destruction, such as the demolition of the Black Boy Hotel, especially when the replacements are so totally without personality.

Probably the novelty of photography led Edwin to make records of subjects which today we would not bother to photograph. Now, when almost everyone must have access to some kind of camera, are we taking pictures that will be as interesting in the future? And to those who are taking such pictures, might we make a special plea to label them? Many were excluded from this book simply because it is not known where they were taken, or, more sadly, who their subjects were.

Michael Payne

One

North Nottingham

Edwin Gordon, 1848–1929. He was born in Brewhouse Yard, where his father was a wharfinger on the canals, (see section 4). For thirty-five years Edwin Gordon was secretary to the Nottingham Patent Brick Company. He was a trustee and vice-president of the Nottingham Mechanics Institution, and a strong supporter of the Liberal cause. He was secretary to the Arkwright Street Baptist chapel and treasurer of the Nottingham Band of Hope.

Edwin Gordon and his family. Taken from a stereoscopic original, this photograph shows E.G. standing with his wife, Emmeline ('Lillie'), on his left, and her mother, Caroline Dann, on his right. In front is his only daughter, Dorothy, who died in 1988 aged 92. His house, Heatherdene, Hartington Road, Sherwood, was built in 1902 for £600, and he lived here until his death.

Portrait of an Edwardian lady. Lillie Gordon sits in the front garden of Heatherdene shortly after its completion. In the upper picture the house on the right is on Burlington Road, showing how little building space had been used at this date (1902). The lower picture, taken from the same spot, probably dates about ten years later.

Hartington Road, Sherwood, 1902. On the left is Elberton House, designed by Watson Fothergill for the bank manager Ernest Gallimore, with Heatherdene the next house on the left. In the distance, over the fields, Hucknall Road can be seen, still lined with trees.

Burlington Road, Sherwood, 1902. Taken from the same point on Burlington Road, we see another Watson Fothergill mansion. To the right would have been Cavendish House, on whose estate this land was developed.

Hartington Road. Heatherdene is on the right, with Elberton House, centre, at the junction with Hardwick Road. Dorothy Gordon rides her bicycle, watched by Edith Gallimore, clearly on an unmade road.

Hardwick Road, Sherwood. Still gated as a private estate, Hartington Road forms a T-junction at the top. The house with two bay windows on the right was known as the Police House, since it was owned by the Constabulary and used as a residence for a senior officer and his family.

Woodville House. Now Woodville Drive at the bottom of Hardwick Road, the big house was hidden in the trees on the right. At the end of the nineteenth century, many of these houses up Mansfield Road sold off their estates for private housing.

Woodville House. One of the few photographs of this house, taken from the garden of Heatherdene in what was previously part of the estate. The old house stands on the left with its stables in the centre of the picture. Today this is the site of Rufford Road.

Cavendish House, Burlington Road. Another of the large houses, now demolished, whose grounds were divided into private housing estates. The four small boys seated on the bank in the top picture are the Gallimore brothers from Elberton House. Cavendish House was probably built in about 1800, and demolished in 1948. One of the last occupants was Captain Athelstan Popkess, who was the centre of a furore in 1950 when as Chief Constable he was controversially suspended by the Watch Committee.

Two housemaids. Domestic servants were considered essential for the running of big houses at this time. The unknown girl on the left is in her afternoon uniform, and Emily on the right is in her best clothes of the fashion of 1912.

Allotments. Many Sherwood people had allotments situated off Hall Street. These were unusual in that they contained brick and tile summerhouses, often with fire grates and sinks. here Mr and Mrs G. Bell have a similar garden in the Hungerhills area.

Chaucer Villas, 1880. Edwin and Lillie Gordon's first house was one of these Victorian villas, off Chaucer Street. The area is now a car park for the Polytechnic. Lillie Gordon is in the front garden.

Chaucer Villas. Another view of the property, which was quite likely rented accommodation. On the right can be seen the new Midland Institution for the Blind on Chaucer Street, which opened in about 1870.

College of Art, 1900. The building opened in June 1865, following the original foundation of a School of Design in Beck Lane 20 years earlier. Two women are leaving the General Cemetery in deep mourning, no doubt after a visit to the grave of someone recently deceased.

Bonington Statue. The portico and statue were donated by Watson Fothergill, in memory of Richard Parkes Bonington, the Arnold-born artist. The statue has been rescued and is now to be seen in the foyer of the Gedling Borough Council Offices at Arnot Hill.

Toll House, Scout Lane. Today Scout Lane is known as Woodthorpe Drive. The story is that owners of sheep who refused to pay the toll drove their animals behind the Toll House in the jitty that still exists.

Scout Lane and Mansfield Road. This view is from the bottom of Woodthorpe Drive, with the park to the left. Opposite are the gates to Woodthorpe House, on Mansfield Road, now the Sherwood Community Centre, with its old lodge on the right. The house was believed to be the oldest in Sherwood and existed before 1774.

The Black Swan, Mansfield Road. The old inn stood at the junction of what is now Villiers Road and Mansfield Road. An old coaching inn, it dates to the eighteenth century, and its trade probably dwindled with the rise of rail travel. It was demolished in 1906.

Elm Avenue, Woodthorpe Park. Looking upwards from Mansfield Road towards Woodthorpe Grange. The trees were planted by the owner, Henry Ashwell, in 1868. They were attacked by Dutch elm disease in the early 1980s and had to be felled. The road also led to Woodthorpe Farm, where there is now a children's playground.

Sheep on Scout Lane. Alongside the railway cutting under Woodthorpe Drive (Scout Lane) a small plot of land was utilized as pasture above Woodthorpe Avenue. Most likely the sheep belonged to Woodthorpe Farm, near the park.

Grange Road, Woodthorpe. The fencing in the foreground over the old railway bridge is still to be seen. The houses along the newly made Grange Road were built in about 1912 and are little changed today.

The Daybrook. In about 1905, when this photograph was taken, the stream still ran through open fields. Edward's Lane bridge is to the rear. It is now mostly culverted following years of liability to flooding, especially after summer downpours.

Jacob's Ladder, Edward's Lane. Now the site of the Five Ways public house, Edward's Lane, then little more than a country track, crossed the Daybrook by an old bridge, called by the locals Jacob's Ladder. The path in the foreground is not far from today's main ring road.

Bagthorpe Hospital, 1905. Now the heart of the City Hospital, the Workhouse, as it was originally, was built between 1899 and 1903. It replaced the City Workhouse on York Street when Victoria Station was built, and to older people the stigma of 'Bagthorpe' was hard to forget. Male and female inmates were described either as able-bodied and of 'good character' or put into two groups of 'bad character'. Healthy inmates were obliged to earn their keep by working in the surrounding fields. The foreground is now Valley Road, the first development of the ring road built in 1925.

Mapperley Brick Works. One of two brick kilns that were fired in rotation throughout the year. The firm has now moved its main works to Dorket Head, Arnold, and since 1995 it has been part of the Ibstock Brick Company Ltd.

THE NOTTINGHAM PATENT BRICK Co.

LIMITED

(Established over Half-a-Century)

Manufacturers of the Celebrated

Nottingham
Wire-Cut
Common

**FACING
BRICKS**

Hand-Pressed

Sand-Faced
(red and multi-coloured)

Multi-Rough
(red and coloured)

A
SPECIALITY

Superior
Wire-Cuts

The Bricks with an arris like Pressed Bricks and

Wire-Cut
Hand-Pressed
Common

for Sewers
Chimneys and
Engineering
Works

THE NOTTINGHAM PATENT BRICK CO., LIMITED

Registered Offices - - 14 GEORGE STREET, NOTTINGHAM

WORKS: Mapperley Hill, Thorneywood, Arnold   SIDINGS: Sherwood L. & N.E.R., Thorneywood L. & N.E.R.

Telegraphic Address: " BRICKS NOTTINGHAM."   Telephone: No. **194** NOTTINGHAM

Mapperley Brick Works. The Nottingham Patent Brick Company had its main works on Woodborough Road between Mapperley Rise and Sherwood Vale (now Woodthorpe Road), to the left and right of this picture. The land to the right of Sherwood Vale was excavated to provide clay, and a railway siding was connected to the line across Woodthorpe Park.

Thackerays Lane, 1910. Top: The old railway bridge carrying the line from Daybrook to Sherwood was demolished in 1975. To the right is where Buckingham Road is today, and the embankment after removal is the site of Raibank Gardens. Below: Looking up towards Saville road; the old lodge to Arno Vale House is on the right. The wall is still the basis of the front garden boundaries of many houses.

Redhill Bridge. Redhill was so steep and punishing for horse-drawn traffic that in 1815 a cutting was made to lower the old North Road. Originally a brick bridge was built for the farms on the hilltop. There have been four bridges in all, the latest dating from 1985.

Redhill, Approaching Nottingham. The hill was less steep on the Ollerton Road side, as seen here looking towards Arnold. The original road was 22 feet wide. In 1927 the road between the sandstone cliffs was widened to 33 feet.

Two

Central Nottingham

The Old Market Square is the largest commercial square in the UK. In 1859 it was measured as 5 acres 2 perches. The market was founded in Norman times by William Peverill. In 1900 it was described as 'surrounded by lofty houses, having good shops with continuous piazzas, banks and hotels, which have now taken the place of the half-timbered buildings that formerly gave such a picturesque appearance'.

Ashmore–Pickering, 1862. One shop surviving from Georgian times belonged to Mr Ashmore, who made umbrellas on his premises, and lived in the little Tyrolean-style apartment above. He later sold his firm to Mr Pickering. Even at this time the premises were dwarfed by their three-storey neighbours. The shop was midway between what we now call King Street and Market Street and is today absorbed into the depths of Debenhams.

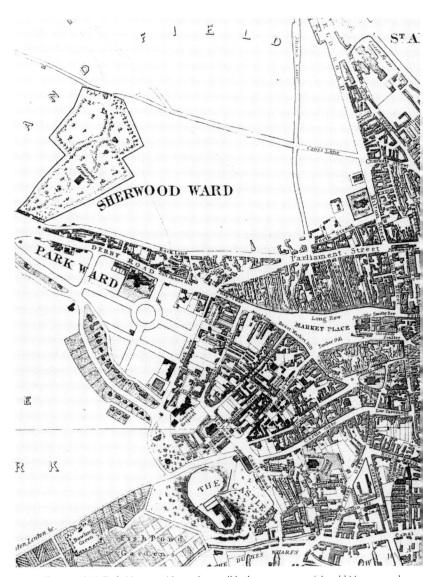

Nottingham in 1844. Early Victorian Nottingham still had many aspects of the old Norman and Saxon boroughs. Parliament Street (once called Back Side) on the north and Park Row to the east still show the line of the old Norman Wall. But the dual nature of the town is appearing: south

of Derby Road, the new wealthy Park Estate is planned, with the Ropewalk and Wellington Circus already constructed. To the north, east, and south, however, the notorious back-to-back housing is emerging, in which four-fifths of the population lived in thousands of slum properties.

Market Square, 1899 from the west. Here we have one of the last photographs of the five-acre Market Square before the advent of the electric tram and the motor car. Market days were Wednesdays and Saturdays. Road works appear to be in progress along most of Long Row, where a traditional ice-cream seller is to be seen. A cab rank is in line with the bottom of Market Street, and the horse-drawn tram on the left travelled the Market Place–Hyson Green–Basford route. The area in the foreground was known as the 'Stones' probably because it was the one area of the square that was paved.

Market Day, 1899. The west end of the Market Square was the site of the old Malt Cross for over 300 years until it was demolished in 1804. From here national pronouncements were made, sermons and political addresses given, and punishments administered. Later it was known as the Stones and was the site of the Pot Market. The central stall is possibly a refreshment tent, with a hazardous-looking brazier quite unprotected. When the old Exchange was demolished in 1926, legend has it that one night an army of rats left the Shambles, seen only by a solitary policeman as it moved up Friar Lane or Clumber Street, according to the particular storyteller.

The Pot Market. At the bottom of the newly formed Market Street all kinds of pottery and china was sold direct from the straw-packed crates in which they arrived.

Market Square, 1904. The introduction of the electric tram greatly affected the market and its stallholders. The new tracks took up more space than the horse-drawn trams, and islands to accommodate poles for the overhead electric cables reduced space. Part of the remedy was to remove the fish, fruit and vegetable markets to Sneinton (and later to the Central Market on Huntingdon Street). With the arrival of the motor car and the building of the Council House, the old Market was finally doomed.

King Street–Long Row, 1904. Trams are now electrified. In the centre is the Black Boy Hotel, designed in 1897 by one of Nottingham's most individual architects, Watson Fothergill. The hotel was not new and Fothergill originally made minor extensions in 1878, but the central tower and balconies are unmistakably in his style. Behind, to the right, can be seen a tower similar to his Nottingham and Notts Bank on Thurland Street.

Long Row East. This street has been known as Long Row since the fourteenth century and may well go back as far as Norman times. Here we look from Skinner & Rook in the foreground, past the balconies of the Black Boy to Watson Fothergill's other building on Long Row, known as Queen's Chambers. At the bottom of King Street, the half-timbered gables, oriel windows, decorated chimneys and turrets have graced this corner of the square since 1897. The colonnade running the length of the row is an ancient feature, a boon to shoppers and newspaper sellers.

Skinner & Rook, No. 1 Long Row and No. 3 Clumber Street. In the mid-nineteenth century William Skinner took over his father-in-law's grocery firm and incorporated a wine and spirit department, including the bottling of imported wines, spirits and beers. A partnership with William Rook in 1860 created what was to be the leading wine and spirit merchants in Nottingham for the following hundred years. Ironically their main rival, Burtons, conducted business from premises opposite on Smithy Row.

High Street, 1899. 'High' is from the Old English 'heagh' meaning 'chief'. The buildings on the left form the rear of the Old Exchange, where in 1799 Joseph Raynor, Nottingham's first postmaster, had his post office. A single letter-carrier, Thomas Crofts, walked round the town each morning and evening with a bell, collecting and delivering mail. By 1815 there were three such carriers. Armitage Bros store is on the right.

Above: Cheapside. Chepe, the old name for market, explains the name. On market days the street was crowded with flower sellers (lower pictures). The shops formed part of the Old Exchange, and the premises to the right of Harrisons was said to be the old Tudor House belonging to the Earl of Mansfield.

Left: Cheapside. The area on this street was traditionally the women's market, and a cross at the junction of Bridlesmith Gate and the Poultry was called either the butter or cheese cross. Farm produce prepared by women was sold here. These flower sellers at the end of the last century were the last to continue the tradition.

The Poultry. A bus for New Basford passes the old Flying Horse Inn, previously known as the Travellers Inn. In the thirteenth century the site was occupied by the Plumptre family, whose house had a garden that extended to St Peter's Gate. The name Flying Horse probably refers to the speed of the coach horses rather than mythology.

Wheeler Gate, 1890. Like Sheep Lane, Wheeler Gate had traffic problems because of its narrowness and in 1892 the shops to the left and beyond became due for demolition. Lambs opposed the compulsory purchase of their premises and the widening was held up for some time before agreement was reached.

Long Row, before 1864. To the left of Deverill's can be seen the side of Sheep Lane, little more than an alley. In 1864, Deverill's and Spybey's properties were demolished to form the new wide Market Street. Dickinsons went through several partnerships to become Griffin and Spalding, now Debenhams.

Wheeler Gate now at its present-day width, but with Friar Lane (to the right) yet to be widened. The Oriental Café was originally a house built in the early seventeenth century. When the property was demolished in 1961, a fine plaster ceiling was saved. Years later it was found in a mason's yard, from whence it mysteriously disappeared..

Exchange Row. The street, which lead to the Poultry, was known until 1800 as Cuckstool Row, because of the ducking stool located at this corner of the square to punish 'scolding' women in the nearby pond.

Victoria Street. From 1868 to 1898 Nottingham's main post office stood at the top of Victoria Street. To the left of the picture is the Imperial Insurance Building. The oriel-windowed building is the office of the architect T.C. Hine, possibly built in a style to challenge Watson Fothergill's George Street office.

High Street, from Bridlesmith Gate. Armitage's Grocery Stores to the right have their summer awnings down, and form the new line of the street when widened in 1890. Farmer's Music Shop removed to Long Row, where it eventually became part of Pearson's store.

Pelham Street, 1900. To the right is Boots main shop, opened in 1892. On the left at first-floor level, over Samuel Page's umbrella shop, is a lifesize statue of Jonas Hanway, who is said to have made the umbrella popular in this country. The poet Byron had an aunt who lived on this street.

Carlton Street, 1897. James Bell, one of Nottingham's leading stationers and map sellers, had a private circulating library. The George Hotel was originally called the King George the Fourth Inn and was built between 1822 and 1823 on the newly formed George Street.

Angel Row, 1900, looking upwards to Chapel Bar. By 1764 there were seventeen ale houses and taverns within the length of Long Row. On the left, below John Perry the jeweller, is the Georgian Bromley House built in 1752. It was the town house of Sir George Smith, grandson of Thomas Smith, who founded Smith's Bank, and an ancestor of Lord Carrington. With its quiet garden at the rear it is the only Georgian house still intact in the square. Henry Barker, the furnishers, was rebuilt and is now the site of the Central Library.

Beastmarket Hill. A street whose name indicates it was near the cattle market when this was held in the square. John Player's original shop, and Elizabeth King, famous for her sausages, are here. St James's Street to the right is one of the few old roads still its original width.

Shoppers outside The Bell, one of Nottingham's oldest Inns. At one time it was half owned by the poor of St Peter's, St Mary's and St Nicholas's churches, who each took a third of half the yearly profit. In 1842, after election meetings ended in a riot, the Chartist candidate took refuge in The Bell.

Friar Lane from South Parade. The street was so named because of the Carmelite House of White Friars founded in 1272 that stood in this area. A tavern is said to have been on the site of the old Moot Hall for centuries. The building seen here was built in the seventeenth century as the Feathers Inn. When the road was widened in 1922 the Moot Hall was rebuilt in mock-Tudor style, and it was this building that was bombed in the air raid of May 1941.

Collins Almshouses. Of all the official vandalism that has hit Nottingham, the loss of the Collins Almshouses is probably the greatest. It was built in 1709 for 'the support of 24 poor men and women'. Pevsner described the building as 'a lovely group, one of the best almshouses of its date in England'. The almshouses were built to form an elegant quadrangle, which contained a large tranquil garden. It was replaced by the horror of Maid Marian Way.

St Peter's Gate. In 1700 the market for vegetables and fruit was removed from Weekday Cross to the front of St Peter's church. Exchange Walk to the left was once known as Farmer's Yard after James Farmer, who owned the drapers business at the Poultry end. It was a private way, and was offered as a road to the square. This never materialized, but today it is a public walkway.

Wheeler Gate known in the fourteenth century as Baxter Gate, Baxter being the old name for bakery. In the fifteenth century the name was changed to Wheelwright Gate. To the left was the St Peter's Hotel, which later became Sisson and Parker, one of Nottingham's main booksellers. On the right is the old general post office on Albert Street, which opened in 1847 and is now Marks & Spencer. In the centre stands the parish church of St Peter, which is chiefly of thirteenth- and fourteenth-century construction.

Lister Gate, 1885. After the opening of the Midland Station attempts were made to have a straight road run to the Market Square. This proved too difficult and the winding access of Wheeler Gate, Albert Street and Lister Gate had to be accepted. Here at the junction with Broad Marsh, flooding was a constant problem and in 1864 the level was raised. The Walter Fountain was built in 1865 to the memory of John Walter, an MP for Nottingham. It stood 50 feet high until further road widening required its removal in 1950.

Lister Gate. Standing with our back to the Walter Fountain we look north towards Albert Street. This short stretch of street was created by clearing property between St Peter's Square and Lister Gate in 1846. To the right is Frederick Clarke's pawnbrokers shop. Today, the camera would have been standing in the café area of the Broad Marsh Centre.

Carrington Street, 1890. At the junction with Canal Street is one of the twelve policemen on point duty in the city. Named after Lord Carrington, the road joins Lister Gate in the distance. To the left is the almost defunct Greyfriar's Gate, a reminder that a Franciscan order of friars once lived in the Broad Marsh area.

Wheeler Gate. By 1892 the demolition of property on the eastern side was complete and the road was at its present-day width.

North-east side of the Market Place. To the left is Bingham's Dining Rooms, which later became the much-loved Mikado Café. In the 1920s it was the setting for many dances and parties, and the elegant wooden staircase is still to be seen in part of Debenham's store. It is not known why the flags are at half-mast.

The Old Exchange, 1895. Built in 1724–6, The New Change was almost a double row of buildings with an internal alleyway. The Shambles contained over sixty butchers' stalls. By 1875 it also included the police office, a museum, and five public houses, as well as many shops and business properties.

Stalls outside the Old Exchange, 1894. Vegetable stalls, as seen here, were soon after removed to Sneinton Market. At the rear can be seen the Prudential Assurance building, King Street, and Queen Street under construction. The Prudential building was designed by Waterhouse in the same terra cotta facing as its London headquarters.

St Mary's church. The parish church of Nottingham, it is, after St Mary Magdalen in Newark, the largest parish church in the county. Although dating back to pre-Norman times the building is almost entirely in the Perpendicular style of the fifteenth century, a time of great prosperity for weaving and spinning towns in England. The west front and clerestory were restored by Sir Gilbert Scott in 1843. To the right of the picture stands one of Nottingham's eight official cab ranks.

Weekday Cross, 1893. Under an 1155 charter of Henry II a market was held here for the tradesmen of Nottingham and Derby on weekdays. This small square was the heart of the old Saxon town, centred on St Mary's church. The Norman town had its large square closer to the Castle, and the silver maces carried before the sheriff still symbolize these two boroughs. Gradually the Saturday Market held in the much larger Market Square overshadowed the weekday event, and may have been a skilful manoeuvre by the Normans to supplant the native English. The old Town Hall can be seen to the left at the end of High Pavement. The London Hotel is in the distance on Middle Pavement.

Opposite below: Criminal courtroom. Sydney Race wrote in his diary: 'it was a musty old place, I felt glad it was coming down. The two courts are remarkably small and one wonders how business was ever carried on in them. The prisoner could almost reach across to the judge in his bench. The dungeons were horrible places—small and damp.'

The old Town Hall. A half-timbered medieval building stood here on Weekday Cross until the 1740s when it was rebuilt 'for doing the business of the Corporation'. Here were held the town assizes and sessions, and council and public meetings, until it was demolished to make way for the MS&L Railway.

Shire Hall, 1870. In 1720 the new Shire Hall was built to replace the 300-year old building used for criminal and civil cases. According to the inscription stone, it was designed by James Gordon. The iron railings were added fifty years later to restrain crowds when public executions took place in front of the building. In 1844, twelve people, including seven children, were killed during a crush after the execution of William Saville, who had murdered his wife and three children. The last public execution took place in 1864.

Civic Court, Shire Hall. In 1876 many improvements were made to the interior, but no sooner had this been completed than a fire destroyed the best part of the work. The damage amounted to £7,000 and restoration work was carried out again. Such was the complexity of the boundary between the town and county that the line of the border actually passed through some courts. One judge complained that if he leant from his seat to speak to the foreman of the jury his head would leave the county.

Headstones. In the exercise yard of the old Debtors' Prison behind the Shire Hall are the headstones from graves of those executed, dating between 1844 and 1877.

Bridlesmith Gate, 1901. Once a main southern road into Nottingham from the top of Drury Hill, which can be seen in the distance. In 1819, when gas lighting was introduced to the town, the road's importance meant that it had the first five of the ten lamps installed. Attempts to have the road renamed Bond Street to add to its fashionable aspirations failed. In spite of the narrowness and sense of the past, it was not in the old Saxon town, but ran parallel with the western boundary.

Middle Pavement. Here at the top of Drury Hill at the junction with Middle Pavement is the old Postern Gate public house. When it was demolished in 1910 the foundations of the old defensive gatehouse were found, and also the vaults giving rise to the old name of Vault Lane for Drury Hill. The Drury Hill post office occupied this site until the advent of the Broad Marsh Centre.

Middle Marsh, 1896. Seen here from the bottom of Drury Hill, Middle Marsh ran at right angles between Broad Marsh and Narrow Marsh. As the name indicates, the area was low and subject to flooding. Its housing was notorious, with back-to-back dwellings built at a density of 500 to the acre, as much for the benefit of stocking frames as for that of the inhabitants. It was in Narrow Marsh in 1787 that the first frames were destroyed by rioters, foreshadowing the Luddite upheavals of the following century. The notice in the Boot Repairer's Shop reads: 'These premises are coming down. Purchased by the M.S.L. Railway. Business will be continued just up Drury Hill.'

Opposite: Drury Hill, 1890 originally called Vault Lane, probably because of Vault Hall, the house at its junction with Low Pavement, which had large rock-hewn cellars. For a time it became Parkyns Lane, named after the family of that name from the village of Bunny. In 1620 it got its final title from an Alderman Drury, then living at Vault Hall. In medieval times it was the main road into the town from the south and at the top there was the Postern Gate. Because of its steepness it gradually lost its importance to Hollowstone, which was lowered and widened in 1740. The loss of this old street when the Broad Marsh Centre was built is still to be mourned. With imagination it could have been incorporated into the scheme, but now it is replaced by a faceless escalator.

Factory Girls, Stoney Street. Between 1851 and 1877, 71 lace factories and 41 warehouses were built in the Lace Market. Adams, Page and Co. built a large warehouse in Stoney Street which was unusual in that it contained rest rooms, tea rooms, a library and a chapel. Here factory girls leave work in the late afternoon. Hollowstone to the right is Nottingham's oldest street, literally cut out of the old sandstone.

The Old Cross Keys, Byard Lane, 1893. Byard Lane was one of the narrow roads that led from the old Anglo-Saxon Borough to the new Norman Borough. It was the west 'sally-port', or entrance into the old walled town. Today's width is probably as it was then. In the photograph, the two postmen on the left may well have been based at the post office then at the top of Victoria Street.

Horse-drawn trams. As early as 1848, horse-drawn omnibuses were being operated by private owners. When the old coaching days were ended by the arrival of the train, these new, compact forms of transport connected the railway stations to the town. The top picture is on Mansfield Road close to Magdala Road. The lower picture shows a tram climbing Derby Road. Such was the steepness of the hill that two additional 'cock-horses' had to be used to help the other two animals.

Tradesmen's Mart, on Lower Parliament Street. This is an unusual building in which tradesmen had their shops at street level and balconied living accommodation above. The Mart was built in about 1770. In 1897 when the Newcastle Street area was cleared the five tradesmen were a broker, an engraver, an umbrella repairer, a boiler and range maker, and a tinsmith.

St George's Hall, Derby Road. Known until recently as Chapel Bar, the road from Derby met the Town Gate at this point. St George's Hall was built in 1854, and was where the famous music hall star, Vesta Tilley, was said to have made her debut at the age of 4. It was demolished in 1901 to make way for the former Co-op Department Store.

George E. Butcher, 1899. Mr Butcher worked from Nos 12 and 13 Smithy Row and described himself as an art jeweller. He was a leading diamond merchant, watchmaker and silversmith. He lived over the shop where both his children were born. Later the firm became Butcher and Swann of Market Street.

Huskinson's Chemists, 1875, at the junction of St Anne's Well Road with Alfred Street Central. It was not unusual for chemists to offer dentistry; Huskinson promised 'painless extractions'.

Armitage's Staff, 1896. Samuel Fox Armitage (1830-1914) was a close friend of the young Jesse Boot and his grocery business supplied Boots original shop. Mr Armitage was a leading member of the Society of Friends and ran his firm on Quaker principles. It was recalled that there were 'two rows of assistants behind the long counters, all dressed in Quaker garb, the men on one side, the women on the other, all in Quaker caps. Everyone knew they could be served at a reasonable price and the "thees" and "thous" were accompanied by a smile.' Here the staff is all male, and seems to be held in order by the large dog in the foreground. The business was eventually overshadowed by Burtons of Smithy Row, but continues today as Pet Produce Manufacturers.

Theatre Square. From 1800 to 1850 this area was used for the Saturday Cattle Market. But carts and speeding carriages coming down Back Lane (Wollaton Street) caused accidents and stampeding cattle, so eventually it was agreed to move the market to Burton Leys, where the Guildhall now stands. Excavations during the making of Market Street revealed part of the old Norman wall, as did works further along Parliament Street when Victoria Station was being excavated. The van declaring 'No Home Rule' puts the date at around 1912.

Theatre Square, 1901. The troops of the South Notts Hussars were probably returning to their camp in Wollaton Park after the Victory Parade at the end of the Boer War (see page 157). To the right can be seen the Clarendon Hotel, forming what was known as Theatre Quadrant. The multi-windowed building to the rear was Whitehall's factory, which was destroyed by fire on 5 August 1905. By 1908 the Hippodrome Music Hall was built here. A poster announces that George Alexander is at the Theatre Royal in *A Debt of Honour*. Later Sir George Alexander, he was a famous actor who made his stage debut in Nottingham in 1879. He frequently returned and was the original John Worthing in *The Importance of Being Earnest*.

Holy Trinity church. The foundation stone was laid in 1840 and eighteen months later the church was consecrated and opened. Its spire stood 177 feet high, but had to be removed in 1941 after air raids made it unsafe. The church was described as a 'daughter church of St Mary's', although Dr Wilkins, the Archdeacon of Nottingham, was angry that Francis Wilford, an evangelical, decided to build Holy Trinity without his agreement. Within ten years Holy Trinity was said to have the largest congregation in Nottingham. Its first vicar was Thomas Hart Davies who drew his parishioners from the Charlotte Street area, one of the poorest in the town.

Trinity Square, 1901. To the extreme left can be seen the east end of Holy Trinity church; beyond it is the newly constructed Victoria Hotel. The square was an important arrival and departure point for carriers' carts for the north. In the centre is the Welbeck Hotel, formerly the Robin Hood and Little John Inn. In 1900 much of Holy Trinity churchyard was taken to form Trinity Square and also to widen Milton Street.

The Mechanics Institute. The Mechanics Institutes were begun nationally by Dr George Birkbeck in the nineteenth century for the education and recreation of artisans or Mechanics, many of whom were illiterate. The Nottingham Institute was inaugurated in 1837 and opened in January 1845. In 1867 a fire destroyed much of the premises, but by 1869 all was restored and improved. It included two large halls, reading rooms, a library, and coffee and billiard rooms, and had over 4,500 members. Many great names appeared here, including Charles Dickens, who gave readings on four occasions. Jenny Lind, John Philip Sousa, Arthur Conan Doyle and Sir Henry Wood were other visitors. The Main Hall ended its days as a cinema, and was closed in 1964.

Milton Street, 1890. The main approach to Nottingham from the north, once known as Boot Lane. It lead to Cow Lane (Clumber Street) and the junction between the two, seen in the distance here, was Cow Lane Bar, a defended entrance to the town, which was reinforced at the time of the Civil War. To the right (off the picture) is Trinity Square, and all the buildings behind the projecting clock, which included the Unicorn Hotel, came down in 1902 so that two lines of tram track could be laid. The Robin Hood and Little John Inn gave way to the Welbeck Hotel.

Milton Street, towards Mansfield Road, 1895. To the left are the railings and trees of Holy Trinity churchyard. The tram lines for the horse-drawn trams are still a single track. A loop to the right enabled trams to pass each other. Many of the shops on the right were soon to come down to make way for Victoria Station and Hotel. Marsdens rebuilt their shop, a well known grocery which also included a café and ballroom.

Mansfield Road from the junction with Charlotte Street on the right, looking north towards St Andrew's church. The tower of the Nottingham Brewery can just be seen. Where the wording 'Linney—Boot Maker' is seen is the corner site soon to be built upon by Watson Fothergill's Rose of England, a public house designed for the Nottingham Brewery. Fothergill excelled in corner site buildings, and this building is an echo of the splendid Black Boy. On the left can be seen the famous Peacock Inn and below that the old Regent Hall.

Charlotte Street. Named after Queen Charlotte, the street fell victim to the building of Victoria Station. The right of way to Glasshouse Street resulted in an elevated walkway over the station being maintained, and the same exit to Glasshouse Street is to be found in the present Victoria Centre. The coming of the railway was a vast undertaking involving the demolition of 1,300 houses and the displacement of more than 6,000 people.

Charlotte Street–Mansfield Road. Almost all the property from the left onwards was demolished in 1897. However, as most of this was some of the worst in Nottingham, the removal could only have been for the better. The old Union Workhouse and twenty public houses also disappeared, the latter explaining the need for the elaborate wrought-iron urinal seen on the left. To the right is Cross Lane, now Shakespeare Street.

Wellington Circus, 1880. One of the most well-to-do areas, named in honour of the Iron Duke, the circus was built in the 1850s. At the rear is Pugin's Roman Catholic cathedral. The houses on this part of the circus were replaced by the Nottingham Playhouse, which opened in 1963.

Forest Road, 1898. Another fashionable area, Forest Ridge, as it was once called, had seventeen windmills along its length. The site of St Andrew's (1871) is said to be that of the old gallows, which gave the district the name Gallows Hill. After the last execution here in 1827 the name was changed to Mars Hill.

Upper Parliament Street. A total contrast to the wealthy houses on the previous page. On the right of this picture between King Street and Market Street was Rigley's Yard. Described as an 'abomination', its clearance in 1881 saw the end of some of the worst slums in England.

Broad Marsh, 1894. Now buried beneath the shopping centre, here was once the settlement of the Grey Friars, whose warden was accused of 'evil living' in both 1500 and 1522. We are standing close to the Walter Fountain, looking towards old Sussex Street. The fireworks sign belongs to Fleeman and Sons, Smallware and General Dealers.

Canning Circus, 1899. The horse trough and drinking fountain would be welcome for the animals after their cruel climb from the square. Beyond is a cabmen's shelter, and the building with the pointed roof was the Corporation Public Weighing Machine, the veracity of which was often doubted. (This point was also known as Toll House Hill.) To the left is the entrance to the General Cemetery, established in 1836 when it lay in open country. Opposite was said to be the Suicides' Graveyard, because of the belief that those who so died had to be buried at a crossroads.

Spaniel Row, a short road between Friar Lane and Hounds Gate. In the eighteenth century, when Nonconformist places of worship had to be registered, the Society of Friends had a meeting place here. Nottingham was visited in 1649 by George Fox, the founder of the Quaker movement, when he was imprisoned for disturbing a service at St Mary's church. While serving his sentence he converted the Sheriff, John Reckless, to his faith.

The Three Tuns, Warser Gate. The reason for taking this photograph is a mystery. The site just demolished is on the corner with Fletcher Gate to make way for I. & R. Morley's new warehouse built in 1899. Some excavations in this area have revealed portions of the old town ditch to the Saxon Borough, but here all that was noted was 'an ancient cellar, left intact, as it affords an eminently suitable place for the storage of yarn'. The horse and cart shows how laborious the carting away of rubble must have been. When completed, this warehouse and counting house employed 243 men and 195 women.

Guildhall, Burton Street, 1898. The new Guildhall was built on the site of the Burton Leys cattle market between 1887 and 1888. In the foreground is the Greyhound Inn and beyond are the Guildhall, the Trinity Church School, and the Mechanics. Victoria Hotel was not yet built.

Guildhall. Although it contained police courts and cells, and the town clerk's office, the building had to be modified because of cost, and central administration was not fully achieved. In 1905 mail from the post box was collected twice on Sundays and eleven times on weekdays between 5.00 a.m. and 11.00 p.m.

High Street, 1890 seen from the end of Clumber Street. To the left of the picture is Boots original shop on Pelham Street, which was rebuilt and extended when the Star Tea Co. came down. This was the site of the Blackamoor's Head. It was here that the body of Lord Byron was brought in 1824. When the funeral procession departed from the inn's yard for Hucknall, the bell of St Mary's tolled, and large crowds turned out to watch. In the centre distance is Bridlesmith Gate.

Right: Boots Original Shop. The premises at No. 6 Goose Gate were originally founded by John Boot as a herbalists. When his son Jesse inherited the shop he added household goods to the stock, and by the mid-1870s was selling proprietary medicines at prices lower than ordinary chemists. By 1883 he controlled ten branches, and had created the forerunners of the modern chain store.

Below: Boots, Pelham Street. With the widening of High Street in 1903, Jesse Boot was able to build a store where his small shop had been ten years earlier. He employed A.N. Bromley to design a neo-Gothic building that occupied the whole of High Street up to his friend Armitage's grocery store. Here the premises are decorated for a royal visit in 1914.

The Arboretum Lake. In 1850 nineteen acres of land were chosen by the Inclosure Commissioners 'to be used for ever as a place of public recreation'. Mr Samuel Curtis of London laid out the grounds, created the small lake, and planted trees, shrubs, and flowers. The Arboretum was opened in May 1852 with refreshment rooms designed by Mr H. Moses Wood (the Corporation Surveyor) with advice from Sir Joseph Paxton of Chatsworth and Crystal Palace fame. Originally the grounds were open to the public on Sundays (after 12.30) and Mondays and Wednesdays, other days being for subscribers only. Eventually, after protest the grounds were open all week and free of charge.

Arboretum Aviaries. A committee of '450 Residents and Ratepayers of the Borough' under the leadership of Mr C. L. Rothera, a solicitor, was formed to build and stock the aviaries. Mr A.N. Bromley designed the cage which was presented to the public in 1890 and contained twenty-three species of birds, including a Virginian nightingale, and surprisingly, two squirrels. So successful was the venture that by 1906 two further cages had been built, including a pool aviary for waterside birds such as kingfishers, gulls, oyster catchers and avocets. In all seventy-nine species of birds were then to be seen.

Theatre Royal, 1898. The theatre was opened in 1865 with the backing of John and William Lambert, the lace dressers, as 'a place of innocent recreation and of moral and intellectual culture'. The design was by C.J. Phipps, very much in the style of Nash's Haymarket Theatre in London, and the cost of the enterprise was £15,000. Here D.H. Lawrence saw Sarah Bernhardt in *La Dame aux Camelias*, a performance which he said so terrified him that he rushed out of the theatre. Nearly all the great names of English theatre have appeared on its stage, from Henry Irving to Julie Andrews. In 1969 the City Council purchased the theatre, saving it from closure. After restoration and improvements it reopened in 1978.

Three

Goose Fair

Goose Fair's origins are lost in time, as are those of all ancient fairs, but it was confirmed by a charter of Edward I in 1284. The original object of selling produce and hiring labour slowly vanished; by the 1870s steam-driven roundabouts had turned the emphasis almost entirely to entertainment. On a Goose Fair Saturday in the early 1900s Victoria Station saw the arrival of sixty special trains, and the Midland forty. Excursions came from as far away as York, Birmingham, Blackpool, Swansea, Liverpool and London. As some of the following photographs will show it was at this time that cinema was born as a fairground entertainment. In this picture, the central roundabout is Green's Cockerels with its unusual pagoda top. It toured from the years 1898–1906 until it eventually ended its life at Coney Island, New York.

Twigdon's Electrograph. Both Twigdon's and Capt Payne's Bioscope are showing the first-ever newsreels of the South African War. Each sideshow had its own generator to provide electricity for projection, and an organ by the entrance. In truth the newsreels were filmed in Hyde Park, but audiences accepted their authenticity when they were also shown 'Local Living Pictures' of Nottingham. This photograph was probably taken in 1899: the Ram Hotel on Long Row was demolished in 1900.

Wall's Fantastascope was next in line to Capt Payne's Bioscope, and had been a 'Ghost and Illusion Show'. At this time it had been bought by Pat Collins who had not yet put his name over the entrance, but we can read 'Collin's Unrivalled Electrograph' on the right, over the electrical control panel. Immediately to the left of this is the generator, and on the left of the entrance a trumpet barrel organ. This worked on a pin-barrel basis and was built by Gavioli of Paris. The figures would have moved to popular music of the day.

Whiting's Venetian Gondolas seen from the top of Wheeler Gate. This was a spinning-top roundabout—the entire top revolving with the gondolas below. To the left can be seen John Collin's 'Gallopers', and on the right his 'Steam Yachts'. In the lower picture the police inspector wearing a shako cap seems to have noticed the photographer, while a brougham turns into South Parade.

John Collins' 'Gallopers' was a steam-driven ride with wooden horses four abreast. The centre would have contained a boiler to drive the roundabout, and the organ. Although called a steam organ, the steam worked the mechanism only and air passed through the pipes, as on a conventional instrument. Ideally, the boiler used best Welsh steam coal, and fuel appears to be stored under the running board. To the right is Whiting's Venetian Gondolas with only a canvas curtain enclosing the side. However, a scene of St Mark's Square is painted on this.

Twigdon's Electrograph being assembled. Three workmen are installing the generator. On the right the two wheels with the barrel between is a 'water dandy' to bring water to the boiler, which was as essential as coal. To the left of the entrance is another Gavioli fair organ, again with moving figures, and a glimpse of a drum which with other percussion instruments would accompany the music. On the left is a Gordon Boy in the uniform of the home.

Long Row Attractions. With our back to King Street we are looking towards Angel Row. Arthur Twigdon also had a gondola ride, but unlike Whiting's gondolas this had a standing top which did not revolve. Next to this is the 'Pigs and Balloons' ride, followed by another 'Gallopers' roundabout, and the last ride is a 'Spring Top' Switchback. On the right are stalls running the length of Long Row in front of the shops and stores.

Wadbrook's Royal Electrograph. These attractions were facing the Old Exchange and were back to back with the previous sideshows. Again they claim to be showing films of the South African War, as is Lawrence's show on the left. Lawrence's poster announces: 'Just arrived, Current Living Pictures Illustrating the Great Paris Exhibition, showing the whole vast buildings passing before you.' The bearded pedlar is probably selling novelty silver balls filled with sawdust and tied with silver string, all on elastic.

The day before the Fair, 1899. Lawrence's Electrograph is not yet open, the organ on the left is covered and a larger curtain covers the entrance. Below this is clearly seen a wheel of the wagon which would form the base of the entrance to the show. Two wagons would be end to end, providing an impressive exterior, and the cinema was a canvas construction behind. Next door Wadbrook's Royal Electrograph declares 'Let Art Prosper' while the Battery on the left of the picture would be a 'Haunted House' type of entertainment.

Children's Corner. At the bottom of King Street in front of the new post office was the traditional area for children's rides. This roundabout is a gentle affair, consisting of small horses and coaches operated manually by the owner standing in the centre. Clearly it is a windy day–the women's dresses are blowing and the canopy of the roundabout is billowing upwards.

Children's Roundabouts. The new post office building and the newly built Prudential offices look down on the two children's rides. The Empire variety hall can just be seen through the left-hand ride. The barrels appear to have been 'spares' from those used to prop up some of the rides, such as Whiting's Venetian Gondolas as on page 102.

We are now in the centre of the Fair. The full legend on the rounding boards seems to be 'P. Collins and Son/Royal Racing/Cockerels/The Greatest/And Most/Elaborate/Machine/Travelling'. The ride appeared at Goose Fair in 1907 and 1908.

Whiting's Venetian Gondolas. The sides of the ride are now boarded in. On the right can be seen barrels supporting the structure, to keep it level against the sloping ground across the Square.

Racing Cockerels. The cross-fall of the Square from Long Row to South Parade can be seen clearly in this picture. The tram lines are kept clear, but it is unlikely that the trams ran through the Fair. In the distance can be seen the gable end of the Mikado Café, where the more well-to-do fairgoers would sit at its windows, drinking afternoon tea and watching the spectacle below.

Fairground living quarters. The following three photographs are a unique record of the wagons and caravans parked in the surrounding streets during the Fair. This is Parliament Street in front of the side entrance to Victoria Station, today the site of Boots Main Store. The caravans on the left and right were known as 'Burtons' and were built by George Orton of Burton-on-Trent. The vans appear to have just arrived, as the horses are being removed from their shafts, prior to being led to graze during the three days of the Fair.

Caravans, Clinton Street West. The third wagon from the right is a bow-topped packing truck. These transported the rides by rail, and some of the larger rides required up to ten for transportation. The two caravans nearest the camera have canvas curtains to protect their paintwork from the sun.

Caravans, Thurland Street. On the right, a splendid luxury wagon with the refinement of a side entrance. To the left of this was a bedroom, and on the right a living room. Built by Orton and Spooner of Burton-on-Trent, this vehicle could have cost £1,000, well over twice the price of a good-quality house.

Gordon Bennett's racing motor cars. It is strange that Gordon Bennett's name is still known. His father owned the *New York Herald Tribune*, and he sent Stanley to find Dr Livingstone in Africa. He also promoted polar expeditions, yachting and motor racing. He died in 1918.

Friday, 4 October 1912. A definite date can be put on this picture of Bostock and Wombwell's menagerie because of the headline of the newspaper seller. A British submarine, the B2, was in collision with the German liner *Amerika* while on a tactical exercise in the English Channel. The submarine was cut in two and fifteen crew members were lost, with only one survivor.

Opposite below: Bostock & Wombwell's Menagerie. A long established part of the Fair. It boasted a 'Magnificent Zoological Collection–Too Numerous to Detail', including a lion called Wallace which may have inspired Stanley Holloway's saga of the Lion and Albert.

Bostock and Wombwell's. Their menagerie, 'Established in 1805', was always situated outside the Talbot Inn, now Yates's Wine Lodge. It was able to support its own brass band which can be seen here playing in top hats. On other occasions they were dressed as beefeaters. The general admission prices, which were 2d. in 1899, had been raised to 6d. by the time this photograph was taken. On the far right can be seen the statue to Queen Victoria, erected in 1905.

Four

Canals, Caves and the Castle

Park Wharf Basin, in about 1870. The River Trent is the natural trading waterway linking Nottingham with the Humber estuary. From 1796 the Nottingham Canal connected the town with the Derbyshire coalfields and indirectly with the great ports of England. Edwin Gordon's father, E.H. Gordon, was registered as a wharfinger and operated a haulage business from one of these wharfs. In 1869 Edwin gave his address as Park Wharf when being registered on the Freemen's Roll at the age of 21. The area was called both Park and Duke's Wharfs in deference to the Duke of Newcastle. Here a coal barge owned by Daniel Brown waits by a gantry at the foot of the Castle Rock.

Duke's Wharf in about 1870. The still-ruined castle was still open to the skyline following the Reform Riots of 1831. The original medieval castle was in ruins when bought by the first Duke of Newcastle, who pulled it down and built a mansion in the classical style between 1674 and 1676.

The Ropewalk, Gordon's Wharf, in about 1870. After the fire of 1831 the Duke of Newcastle received a large sum of compensation from the county, but did not use it to repair the house. At one time it was suggested that the building be turned into a prison. Today this area is part of the Park Estate (see page 112).

The Hermitage. The old caves along the south side of the Park have given rise to many fanciful theories. There are tales of chapels, Papist holes, and the map of 1844 even refers to 'Druidical Remains'. The house above was built by John Leavers and was known romantically as The Hermitage.

Hermitage Caves, Castle Boulevard. The caves were most likely to have been used as storerooms, and fish from the river Leen were cleaned for use in the Castle. The many small holes are thought to be the equivalent of dovecotes, where unfortunate birds were kept for winter food.

Castle Boulevard Caves. Some of the new houses in the Park Estate utilized the old sandstone caves in their gardens as stores and even summer houses. Most have been destroyed or lie hidden beneath the industrial developments along Castle Boulevard.

Hamilton Drive, The Park, in 1889/90. Much of this area had been allotments before being built upon, and this photograph is taken from Fishpond Drive, named after the Fishpond Gardens. Hamilton Drive veers to the left, where houses are under construction. This view is not far from the old Ropewalk seen on page 110.

Francesca on the Nottingham Canal. Further to the west from the Park Wharfs lay the boatyards of the Nottingham Canal. Here barges would be repaired and even built, as can be seen to the left. The splendid cabin steamer Francesca appears in many of Edwin Gordon's photographs, but her owner is not known.

Brewhouse Yard once contained the brewhouses to the Castle, and by a quirk of history was a small township outside the rule of Nottingham. It became inhabited by many criminals who found it ideal to be outside the town's laws. This was brought to an end in 1877 by the Borough Extension Act.

Park Wharf Basin, in 1880. The Castle had been rebuilt and opened by the Prince and Princess of Wales in July 1878. However, the canal caused much offence to the new inhabitants of the Park, who spoke of its filthy condition and stench. By 1892 the responsibility lay with the Great Northern Railway, and solicitors to the Duke of Newcastle wrote to the Railway saying that it was nothing less than an open sewer. As a new low road was required 'to meet the new road known as Gregory Boulevard' and to avoid the hills of Ilkeston and Derby Roads, the Park Wharves were finally filled, the canal diverted, and Castle Boulevard created by 1884.

Canal Warehouses. Although Castle Boulevard brought road traffic to the Midland Station more efficiently than before, the Nottingham Canal was still a means of bulk transport. The double-gabled premises of Fellows, Moreton & Clayton was a transhipment warehouse between the canal and Trent. Here goods were transferred from the narrow boats of the canal to the wider river boats of the Trent and vice versa. The connection was made in the tunnel under the building. Gill & Bibbey's warehouse has gone, and to the extreme left can be seen the left arm of the canal which flows alongside the present Trent Navigation Warehouse.

Castle Terrace, in 1890. At this spot it is usual for photographs to be taken of the Castle Gateway. Here we look in the opposite direction towards Castle Terrace at the foot of Standard Hill. The public house is named after one of King Charles I's staunchest opponents, Colonel John Hutchinson, a leading Parliamentarian in the Civil War, and a member of the committee that tried and sentenced the King. The premises around the public houses were mostly lodging houses, and possibly a brewery for the Inn, although a singing teacher and a 'Collector at the Hide and Skin Market' also lived here.

Opposite below: Wollaton Village is little changed today, apart from the removal of ivy from St Leonard's church. To the left is the Admiral Rodney, and on the right cottages that are thought to be medieval. Possibly they were connected with the old Manor House of which traces were found beneath the old rectory behind the church.

Old Gateway, Wollaton Hall today left in isolation because of the building of Middleton Boulevard, but at this time the Hall could be seen in the distance. To the right was the Nottingham Canal which was positioned to help Wollaton Colliery in its struggle for sales of coal against the mines of the Erewash valley.

South Gate to Wollaton Hall. In 1841, the day after the burning of Nottingham Castle, rioters fired a silk mill at Beeston and then marched on Wollaton Hall. By now the militia were ready, and they were repelled, with arrests taking place which brought an end to the troubles.

Beeston Lane was once a main road from Beeston to Derby Road across the Highfield estate. The estate was bought by Jesse Boot in 1920, where he intended to build another Bournville. Later he donated the land with £50,000 to found the university, which has now absorbed the road into its campus.

Five

Trent Bridge and the River

Old Trent Bridge was known in the Middle Ages as Hethbeth Bridge, and was built early in the fourteenth century. It had seventeen arches, was 668 feet in length and was constructed mainly of local sandstone on top of oak piles driven into the river bed. The bridge was later widened from its original 12 feet to 20 feet, but by the mid-nineteenth century was both unsafe and inadequate for the traffic it had to carry. The River Trent in summer, as here, could be low enough to walk over on the stones of the river bed, but in winter it could flood from West Bridgford to the Meadows.

Trent Bridge from the City side. In 1868 the Town Council approved a plan to build a new bridge from the southern side of the river and further downstream from the old one. The newly appointed borough engineer, M.O. Tarbotton, prepared designs, and the cost was to be £30,000. In the trees on the Bridgford side the police station can be seen.

Trent Bridge from the Bridgford side. The old bridge was to the left of the new one, and a memorial stone was laid in July 1869. The council had the imagination to include a lead time capsule containing articles and items for discovery by a future generation. The construction of the new bridge took two years, and it was opened on 25 July 1871.

Town Arms and water works, in 1901. On the left can be seen the old engine, pumphouse, and chimney to the water works which were demolished when the new embankment was made on the north bank. Beyond these stands the new Town Arms which was built on the site of an earlier public house.

Trent Bridge traffic, in 1901. Surprisingly the Town Council was much criticized for the excessive width of the new bridge, which was considered by many an extravagance. By now the amount of traffic to be seen on the bridge would seem to merit the width of 40 feet, over three times that of the original. Through the arch on the left can be seen the approach to the old Navigation Bridge.

Cattle crossing Trent Bridge. Sheep and cattle walked to market at East Croft until as recently as the 1920s. A farmer in Thrumpton recalls Mr Towers of that village rising at 4.00 a.m. to drive his cattle to London Road, then walking home again to be at his plough by 1.00 p.m. This view is from the Bridgford side with Turney's leather factory chimney above the cart to the right. Logically, this factory was close to the cattle market and abattoir.

Trent Bridge–Town Arms, in 1896. The Nottingham and District Tramways Company began operating in 1878 with two services. These were from St Peter's church to Trent Bridge via Carrington Street and Arkwright Street, and from St Peter's church to London Road via Carrington Street and Station Street. Thus both railway stations, the Midland and the Great Northern on London Road, were served by the eight trams initially employed. From West Bridgford, a large group of cyclists cross into Nottingham.

Trent Bridge Police Station. This picture shows the junction of Loughborough Road and Bridgford Road, with the police station on the right and the police house on the left. The police officer living here had the remains of old Trent Bridge in the garden, which at one time were wired in and used as chicken houses. On the right can be seen the gates to Trent Bridge Cricket Ground.

Police House, in 1901. Although probably taken on a Sunday morning, it is worth remembering that traffic over the river was to increase so greatly that by 1926 Trent Bridge had to be widened to twice its original width. The police station and house were demolished when a new roundabout was built to regulate traffic in 1952.

Two Trent Bridge Inns, in 1885. Until changed in the 1870s, the boundary between West Bridgford and Nottingham passed through the Trent Bridge Inn. When the Mickleton jury beat the bounds, it was said they climbed in one window and fell out of the other. The famous cricket ground was established in 1838 by William Clarke, who married the inn's landlady.

Lovers' Walk, in 1901. To prevent seasonal flooding by the Trent, the Embankment was built, together with this walk on the south bank. The area on the right is now occupied by County Hall.

Trent Bridge, south bank. To the right is A.J. Whitty's boat yard, and next to that the
Nottingham Rowing Club house established in 1862, and beyond that Nottingham Forest
football ground. A summer scene: there are rowing boats for hire, and one of Mr Whitty's
pleasure steamers is en route for Colwick Park.

The same view in winter when the pleasure steamers were moored with their landing stages
removed from the summer position on the north side of the river. The football ground has been
enlivened by advertisements for the Empire Music Hall and Football Chat. The large central
chimney belonged to Hall's glue and bone works, processing another by-product of the
cattle market.

Whitty's boat yard. A.J. Whitty's boat-building firm began on Meadow Lane in 1862 but soon moved to this position on the south bank of the Trent. In 1885 Mr Whitty introduced a summer service to Colwick Park which became very popular. Closest to the camera is his steamer *Queen* and next to the bank the *Empress*.

Colwick steamer. *Sunbeam* was the first of Whitty's steamers, built at his Meadow Lane yard in 1886. She had a timber hull, was 65 feet in length and could carry 166 passengers. As part of her attractions a trio of musicians played the concertina, the violin, and the harp, which can be seen on the upper deck.

Colwick steamer. *Sunbeam* was so successful that a sister ship, the Queen, was launched in 1888. Again wooden in construction, she was 70 feet long and could seat 200 passengers. The trip to Colwick was 2d. at the open ends of the boat and 3d. on the upper deck.

Old reservoir, Trent Bridge. On the city side of the river, the old water works were demolished to make way for the new embankment. Here we see the old reservoir just before it was filled in, with Turney's Factory at the right rear.

A houseboat near Colwick. The Trent saw a golden age between 1880 and 1910. At Colwick Park, a band played for dancing, and the pleasure gardens provided food and drink as well as a menagerie. Here a houseboat has its own moorings and jetty. The red ensign would suggest an association with the Royal Navy.

Great Northern Railway bridge. Further upstream, the Great Northern line crosses the Trent to Radcliffe-on-Trent. Rectory Junction is on the Netherfield side of the river, with signals for Nottingham, Colwick Yards and Gedling.

Bucket dredger at Wilford, in 1900. The Trent Navigation Company employed a bucket dredger to keep clear a channel for navigation, and also help flood prevention. The river was dredged by a conveyor belt of buckets that chuted its contents onto barges on either side. The river bank opposite was soon to become the Victoria Embankment, and we are almost opposite the present-day Wilford Grove recreation grounds. The Wilford Great Northern railway bridge can be seen at the rear right.

Looking towards Trent Bridge from the same position: on the extreme left is Trent Bridge in the distance, and the trees of Lovers' Walk. At this time the boundary included this part of the south bank in the city of Nottingham. It crossed the river near the point where the suspension bridge was to be built in 1906. The dredger not only cleared a channel for shipping on the river, but the gravel it removed was sold commercially.

Wilford church and the dredger. Looking more as if it is on the Seine than on the Trent, with bowler-hatted men sunning themselves, the bucket dredger continues its work. Edwin Gordon would have been especially interested in the dredger, as he had a small business on the Trent near Gainsborough where the fine river sand was dredged, dried and sent to the silver works in Sheffield where it was used in the polishing process.

The Trent at Wilford. Opposite the Kirke White Cottage, the meandering course of the Trent can be seen before widening took place and the embankment was built. The low banks and shingle spars obviously attracted fishermen and paddlers, but were no defence against the river when it rose. Flooding was almost an annual event, and as late as spring 1947 even the Midland Station was reached by flood waters. Since then the widening of the river and further embankments have prevented a repetition.

Kirke White Cottage, Wilford. Henry Kirke White is a poet little remembered today. He was born at Wilford, reputedly in this cottage, and died while an undergraduate at St John's College, Cambridge, aged 21. He was befriended by the then Poet Laureate, Robert Southey, so reviled by Byron.

Wilford church. At this time, Wilford was a picturesque riverside village. The church of St Wilfrid, the rectory and the whitewashed Ferry Inn 'still make a pleasant group', wrote Nikolaus Pevsner in 1951. Today the Clifton bridge and its approach roads almost elbow it in to the river.

Colwick: the steamer *Empress*. By 1900 Whitty's trips to Colwick required a third vessel and the *Empress* was the most impressive of all. She had a music room which contained a baby grand piano. The boats left Trent Bridge every twenty minutes from 2.00 p.m. until 9.40 p.m. From Colwick Landing, the twenty-minute service continued until the last boat left at 10.15 p.m. It may be that Mr Whitty himself is at the helm, with the handsome ship's brass bell before him. The *Empress* ended her days with honour, and was one of the 'little boats' in the 1940 evacuation of Dunkirk, being sunk on her second trip across the Channel.

Wilford Main Street. In 1901 the population of Wilford was 554, with a lord of the manor at Clifton Hall. The second cottage from the left was one of the two shops in the village owned by 'John H. Chapman, Licensed to sell tobacco and cigars'.

The Bee Bank at Wilford. In 1875 the Trent 'overflowed its banks and caused great destruction of property and some loss of life'. One of the first attempts to prevent this recurring was the building of the Bee Bank. Nottingham is seen on the extreme left.

Six

West Bridgford

'New' West Bridgford. Until 1880 West Bridgford was a small agricultural village of about fifty houses and less than 300 inhabitants, all under the ownership of Mr John Chaworth Musters. Seeing the expansion of Nottingham, and the need for good-quality housing areas, in 1881 Musters decided to sell much of his land between Musters Road and Loughborough Road for housing development. West Bridgford has never had a railway station, and the Grantham Canal merely passed by the area without any effect upon the rural life of the village. All this changed when 'New' West Bridgford quickly spread as a dormitory for overcrowded Nottingham. Large new houses appeared, such as these on Loughborough Road by which the exotic parade of Barnum and Bailey's circus passes in 1898.

Lady Bay Bridge. At this time this was a narrow hump-back bridge with a canal worker's cottage at its side. Lady Bay was looked down upon by the other side of West Bridgford, and was nicknamed the 'tanner' side by the 'bob' people.

Radcliffe Road. By 1901 the population of West Bridgford had risen to nearly 7,000, yet this road was still thinly housed. Lady Bay Bridge can be seen through the old railway bridge, which bears the painted slogan: 'Dixon and Parker, Boys' and Youths' Tailors—Cheapest and Best.'

Holme Road was still a country lane reached by crossing the canal bridge. When the Lady Bay Estate was developed in 1889, the most expensive building plots were here on Holme Road, with its views of the river, and also on Trent Boulevard.

Coronation Avenue Railway Bridge, in 1901. More or less on the site of today's Wilford Meadows School was this gentle walk from Wilford Lane across to the village. The embankment and bridge were for the newly opened Great Central Railway, running from Victoria, which cut such a swathe through south Nottingham.

Lady Bay Lock was the meeting point between the Grantham Canal and the Trent, with the lock-keeper's house nearby. The Grantham Canal, which opened in 1797, was a wide waterway, and boats could travel in pairs. Two can be seen side by side on the right of the picture. This part of West Bridgford would still have been in the city of Nottingham, and the lack of housing enables us to see the railway bridge over Radcliffe Road from the opposite side to the view on page 138. West Bridgford has never had a railway station, as Chaworth Musters, refused to give permission for one when the line was being built.

Holme Lock. This is the first lock on the length of the River Trent. The serpentine river was always difficult for navigation at this point and meandered behind the lock-keeper's house. Today that part of the river has become the lake in Colwick Country Park. River traffic still passes through the lock (which was rebuilt in 1922 by the Corporation), although the lock-keeper's house was burnt down in 1939. The rowing course of the National Water Sports Centre is now to the left of the picture.

Albert Road. More than any other picture, this shows the old West Bridgford before the land sales of 1881. The houses at the left are at the bottom of Albert Road, which bends to the left. Davies Road and Gordon Road are now on the right. The gas lamp would have been one of the first in West Bridgford.

Rural Bridgford. Today this is Tudor Square, with the camera standing at the east end of Rectory Road. The road sign for Exchange Road is almost exactly where the present post office stands.

Musters Road in 1899, at the junction with Melton Road and Rectory Road on the right. On the right are the six almshouses built in 1892 by Catherine Peatfield, widow of Revd John Peatfield, 'who was 29 years curate of this Parish'.

Melton Road. From the same point we now look south-east down Melton Road, where through the railway bridge is still unspoilt countryside. At this time Edwin Gordon lived on Henry Road and the cyclist is Lillie, his wife.

Musters Road Methodist church was opened in May 1899 at the time when housing was gradually moving south down Musters Road. It was thought that the church would be centrally placed in 'New' Bridgford, but as the area developed more to the east, another Methodist church followed on Trent Boulevard in the early 1900s. A proposal for a third church on Gordon Road never materialized. The empty area in the foreground is now the site of the Epperstone Court.

Musters Road School. Built originally as a Board School, it opened in April 1895 with Mr E.J. Eley as headmaster. There were 141 children registered, many of whom were at a school for the first time. The design of the school was far from satisfactory, and there were complaints of bad lighting and ventilation, as windows were high and only on one side of the classrooms. By 1900 the attendance was over 500 and the school was promoted to become a Higher Grade School.

Old Costock Mill. The railways enabled cyclists to carry their machines into the countryside, and explore villages farther afield. The four friends are posed by the old box mill at Costock. The box mill, already derelict, was of the type once to be seen along Forest Road, Nottingham, where there were seventeen. Lillie Gordon is second from the right. Her bicycle and the one on the extreme right do not have the luxury of hand brakes.

Rolleston Junction. This station was on the main Nottingham–Lincoln line, but here the train is standing on the branch platform, most likely bound for Southwell, although a few trains ran through to Mansfield. The engine appears to be No. 1253, an 0-4-4 tank engine designed by Samuel White Johnson, who is buried in the church cemetery, Forest Road.

Wilford Lane, in 1901. At the turn of the century Sir Jesse Boot built the stone and wood building he called Plaisaunce on Wilford Lane. Here it can just be seen behind the fencing. Senior staff from Boots were invited at weekends with their wives and families to enjoy its grounds.

Plaisaunce boasted recreation grounds, tennis courts and children's amusements. Later the Boots Brass Band & Choral Society met here, as well as the Boots Athletic Club. The boy scouts also held parades, demonstrations and inspections.

Barnum and Bailey's Parade. The famous American circus made the first of several visits in 1898. Barnum had died in 1891 worth 5 million dollars but the show continued. The flamboyant publicity, typical of American show business, resulted in parades such as this one along Loughborough Road.

(Overleaf)

Equally impressive would have been Buffalo Bill's Wild West Show, which visited West Bridgford in 1883 and, as shown here, in 1903. With his troupe of Indians, Mexicans, cowboys and scouts, Buffalo Bill attracted crowds of seven thousand at each performance. The spectacle included the Capture of the Deadwood Mail Coach by Indians, the Pony Express, and a Buffalo Hunt. Most famous of all was Annie Oakley, heroine of *Annie Get Your Gun*. The *Nottingham Daily Guardian* wrote: 'She is a wonderful shot and notwithstanding a brisk breeze which caused the clay pigeons to curl away, and a bad light, she made few mistakes'. The show was staged on the Radcliffe Road showground, where the ill-fated Industrial Exhibition was built (and burnt down) the following year.

NOTTINGHAM.   TWO DAYS ONLY.   MONDAY & TUESDAY
OCTOBER 19 & 20.
GROUNDS, RADCLIFFE-ROAD, NEAR TRENT BRIDGE.

BUFFALO BILL'S
WILD WEST

And Congress of Rough Riders of the World.

The World's Greatest Educational Exhibition,

EMBRACING AS IT DOES THE

HERO HORSEMEN
OF ALL NATIONS

NOW TOURING THE PROVINCES
VISITING THE PRINCIPAL CITIES AND
GREATER RAILWAY CENTRES ONLY.

FOUR SPECIAL TRAINS,
1,300 MEN AND HORSES.

THE ENTIRE GRAND PROGRAMME
will positively be presented
undivided and uncurtailed
TWICE DAILY, RAIN or SHINE.

THE GREAT
WILD WEST
— AND —
WILD EAST
Now United Hand-in-Hand.

**The Orient
& Occident**
RIDE
Shoulder to
Shoulder
IN THE
**GREAT
ARENA**
100
American
Indians,
Chiefs,
Warriors,
Bucks,
Squaws &
Papooses.

Step by step the path-finders
encircled the globe. Note the end-
less array of stirring attractions.
Russian Cossacks, Bedouin Arabs,
American Cowboys, Indians, Go-
bans, Western Girls, Mexicans,
Johnny Baker, Bucking Bronchos,
Stage Coach, Emigrant Train,
Scenes of Border Life on the
Western American Plains.

The World's Mounted Warriors
Headed and personally
introduced by
Col. W. F. CODY
("Buffalo Bill.")

Historic Military Spectacle, The
BATTLE OF SAN JUAN HILL
Introducing Roosevelt's Rough Riders.
The vast arena illuminated at night by Two Special
Electric Light Plants.

TWO PERFORMANCES EVERY WEEK DAY.
Afternoons at 2. Evenings at 8. Doors open at 1 & 7 p.m.
ONE TICKET ADMITS TO ALL ADVERTISED ATTRACTIONS.

PRICES OF ADMISSION:
1s., 2s., 3s., 4s.; Box Seats, 5s. and 7s. 6d.
Children under ten years half-price to all except the 1s. seats.

All seats are numbered except those at 1s. and 2s. No Tickets under 1s. sold
in advance.

Tickets at all prices on sale on the grounds at hours of opening, and tickets
at 4s., 5s., and 7s. 6d. on sale at 9 a.m. on the day of exhibition at
EDGAR HORNE, PIANO WAREHOUSE, 27, LISTER-GATE.
A FREE ENTERTAINMENT FOR EVERYBODY
Visiting the Exhibition Grounds at 11 a.m., Preliminary Open Air Concert by the
Famous Cowboy Military Band and other interesting Features.
WILL EXHIBIT AT NEWARK TO-DAY, LOUGHBOROUGH, OCT. 21.

Buffalo Bill's Wild West Show.

150

Seven

Skegness and Soldiers

'Nottingham-on-Sea'. Photographs of Skegness in a book on Nottingham are not as illogical as it might seem, especially when thinking about Victorian times. The craze for taking the waters and sea-bathing, once the province of the wealthy, was changed radically by the coming of the railways. Just as Blackpool served the millions of Lancashire, and Brighton those of London, so Skegness became the seaside holiday mecca for Nottingham. In 1873 Skegness was described as 'a retired watering place'. But in 1874, following the building of the railway from Nottingham, August Bank Holiday saw ten thousand day trippers visit the resort. Of all the Lincolnshire resorts, Skegness was most successful in providing accommodation and amusements for both working people and the more genteel. By 1883 nearly a quarter of a million visited Skegness annually. Amusement parks were an important part of the town's facilities, and here on the North Shore is one of the early switchbacks, which stood from 1885 to 1911. Soon to follow was Billy Butlin's Arcade, and later his revolutionary holiday camp.

Lumley Road, Skegness. In addition to the annual week's holiday, the introduction in 1883 of the half-day for shop assistants brought about another phenomenon. Half-day holiday societies arranged regular day trips to Skegness for staff from Nottingham shops and stores. Lumley Road is a main shopping centre leading to the Clock Tower, a focal point on the seafront for all kinds of activities from the Salvation Army to illuminations.

The Victorians had a mania for piers, and there was great rivalry between resorts to build longer and more splendid constructions. The Earl of Scarbrough backed the Skegness Pier Company in offering £50 for the best design. The winners were Clarke and Pickwell, whose scheme included this impressive entrance up a flight of eight steps to an ornate toll office with shopping kiosks on either side.

Clarke and Pickwell's Skegness Pier was 1,854 feet in length, making it one of the longest in the country. Here we see the large pier head, where from 1882 onwards the Skegness Steamboat Company ran trips to Hunstanton and the Norfolk coast. Shelters on the pier were built in pairs. On the sands patient donkeys line up to give children rides.

Pier Theatre. Entertainments varied from daring men who dived off the end of the pier to shows in the Pavilion. In August 1880 it was possible to see 'Captain Slingsly, ventriloquist, Walter Howard, banjoist, and Signor Isidore Corelli in *Silent Sorcery*.' There was also an orchestra twice daily, and on Sundays Sacred Concerts at 8.00 p.m. On the right, wearing a tam o'shanter, is Lillie Gordon, with her daughter Dorothy.

Skegness Pier was the place to show off the latest fashions, and the two women at the centre of the picture wear dresses and hats of the highest mode. On the left black umbrellas and cloaks keep off the sun for older women. Little concession was made to the heat, and even the children are covered from head to foot. On the right attention is focused on a band concert. This photograph and that opposite show, touchingly, two ways of life gone for ever.

The Regiment of the South African Contingent of the South Notts Hussars is welcomed back to Nottingham on 10 June 1901. The mounted troopers in full-dress uniform assemble here on King Street before marching into the Square to an official welcome from the High Sheriff, Sir John Robinson. The furthest mounted figure in the centre is the Regiment's commanding officer, Colonel Sir Lancelot Rolleston. At the top of King Street, Albion Chambers are under construction, and shopgirls watch from the windows of the new Jessops store.

Soldiers on Thurland Street. On 27 May 1902 the Regiment again paraded in the market place for the 1902 training. Some 495 officers and men were on parade. These men may have been recruits in the new service drab, and again they were camped in Wollaton Park. In both pictures the Watson Fothergill Bank is to the right, with Thomas Danks Showrooms beyond.

The unveiling of the South African War Memorial took place on 26 March 1903. In attendance are men of the Volunteer Battalions of the Nottingham and Notts. The Memorial was presented to the city by Mr T.I. Birkin and was unveiled by General Lord Methuen. Prayers were said by Bishop Hamilton Baynes. In attendance were representatives for the Sherwood Rangers, South Notts Hussars, and the Robin Hoods.

Bibliography

Adamson, Simon H., *Seaside Piers*, Batsford; Beckett, John, *The Book of Nottingham*, Barracuda Books; Brand, Ken, *Watson Fothergill*, Nottingham Civic Society; Chapman, Stanley, *Jesse Boot of Boots the Chemist*, Hodder and Stoughton; Gray, Duncan, *Nottingham–Settlement to City*, Nottingham Co-operative Society Ltd; Nottingham Historical Film Unit, *Victorian Nottingham*, Iliffe and Baguley; Pevsner, Nikolaus, *Nottinghamshire*, Penguin; West Bridgford and District Local History Society, *Aspects of West Bridgford's History*.

Soldiers in Milton Street. Eleven years later men of the Robin Hood Rifles march to Victoria Station, almost certainly for embarkation for France. The picture is taken from the first floor of the Mechanics Institute. It is ironic to think that the crowds here might well have been cheering King George and Queen Mary on their visit to Nottingham, less than two months before the outbreak of the First World War.

Acknowledgements

Sincere thanks to Sheila Cooke, Dorothy Ritchie and the staff of the Nottinghamshire Leisure Services Local Studies Library. Also, Graham Downie of the Fairground Association of Great Britain, Stephen Best, R.H. Bird, Ken Brand, Judy and Jeff Briggs, Harold Harper, Geoffrey Oldfield, Dick Venner of West Bridgford Library, John Wing, and Sarah and Roger Payne.